# Table of Contents

Introduction ................................................................. 1

Chapter 1: Psychic Vampires ........................................... 4

Chapter 2: Characteristics of Energy Vampires .................. 14

Chapter 3: Types of Energy Vampires .............................. 24

Chapter 4: The Empath and the Energy Vampire ............... 36

Chapter 5: Symptoms of Energetic Vampirism ................... 44

Chapter 6: How Energy Vampires Take Energy ................. 59

Chapter 7: How To Deal With Energy Vampires ................ 69

Chapter 8: Characteristics of an Empath .......................... 77

Chapter 9: How To Embrace Your Intuitive Gifts ............... 86

Chapter 10: The Empath's Way Of Life ........................... 103

# Introduction

We live our daily lives just going about our business, yet often fail to think of the concepts that haven't crossed our paths. Many people haven't heard of or fully understand the idea of psychic or energetic vampirism. They feel it is some type of concept of folklore or an ideation that isn't real and that is a fictional concept you might find in vampire stories, movies, books, or other paraphernalia. However, the concept of energy vampirism is very real and takes place not only on a daily basis, but happens momentarily every second of our lives and existence. It happens 'everywhere', and yet it's something that many people rarely think about until it happens to them in a major way.

Psychic vampirism is a huge problem in society though it's rarely talked about, but the issue still exists, and people have to deal with or handle those who are there to steal energy or take another person's life force. Psychic vampires are all around us and are very real. You often hear of the concept 'energy takers,' but may not fully understand what that means or what it's referring to. Psychic vampirism can have harrowing effects on a person's life, their lifestyle, and within their current reality. People who take energy can have an extremely negative effect on their target victims and it can create a snowball effect that can harm someone's life in repetitive ways. These predators lurk everywhere amongst us, but people rarely want to believe they exist, and do not care about the damaging effects they can have on a person and their life. A psi vampire can hide amongst normal people and cause a host of issues for someone if they decide to strike and turn someone into their victim.

You often hear of the concept 'energy takers,' but may not fully understand what that means or what it's referring to. Psychic vampires are beacons of negative energy who harbor negative thoughts and ideations towards others. they hold no positive notions for others and are takers, not givers. It's important to learn how to protect yourself from a psychic vampire and not let them affect your life in a major way.

Empaths are highly intelligent individuals who exist in this world as people who do good and give energies to others and are often known as peacemakers. Psychic vampires dance a fine dance with empaths for they do not hold a liking to empaths and far often will do anything in their power to ruin or bring down an empath or even destroy them. Psychic vampires often target empaths to feed off of due to their high energy and are jealous of the great qualities an empath possesses.

Empaths are extremely positive good people who are harbingers of good and positive energies. They seek to help and heal others and do their best to bring peace and harmony wherever they are at. Empaths are the opposite of energy vampires, and many energy vampires have a secret and open dislike and even hatred for empaths. Empaths and energy vampires perform a fine dance together as one is a beacon of positivity, while the other is one of negativity hatred and darkness.

The psychic vampire seeks to steal from the higher energy empath, while the higher energy empath seeks to do good and to heal and to help others. They both encounter each other as dual opposites who can't co-exist with each other due to the ill nature of the energy vampire. The energy vampire will do anything it can to bring down, hurt, ruin or even destroy the empath, while the empath will do anything in his or her power to heal and help the energy vampire. Protecting yourself from the targets of the energy vampire is something you'll learn to know and learn in order to be able to thwart its attacks and bad intentions.

# Chapter 1

# PSYCHIC VAMPIRES

## What are Psychic vampires

Psychic vampires are all around us. They come in many different forms from a random negative energy vampire to a person that can actually take someone's energy very willingly using their metaphysical or psychic supernatural abilities. There are many kinds of psychic vampires that exist in society. What is an energy vampire? An energy vampire or energetic vampirism is the negative aspect of taking someone's energy willingly or sometimes unconsciously, without the other person's permission or knowledge.

Energy vampires are all around us and they are everywhere. Energy vampirism is something that some people are aware of, but that the general population really has no knowledge of or thinks about on a regular basis. Most people aren't introduced to this negative aspect and these types of interactions take place on a regular basis anyway and most have little knowledge of this. The reason for this is because these people aren't empaths or don't have a large amount of energy around them, just floating around them, or in space for others to notice or take. In other words, these people simply aren't high energy beings or possess a certain amount of positive energy, that those who do may experience as a result of this.

Energetic exchanges between individuals are extremely important and are a major part of existing in this universe. They are rarely talked about, and most people aren't consciously aware of energetic actions that are going on around them. There are some who are aware, though they may not do much about it. Energy is around and about us everywhere and energetic interactions take place on a very normal basis. Healthy energetic interactions consist of a person or people giving and taking energy in a normal and healthy manner. Unhealthy energetic interactions generally consist of a person or people not having a mutual exchange of energy between them, and one taking the energy or life force of another by dominating, putting them down, creating a hostile environment, or using other tactics in order to establish a way to steal their energy or life force.

There are many negative aspects of spirituality that can be present in someone's life. Dark energy or vampirism is something that is common amongst those who practice a negative form of being spiritual. There is a true and defined form of darkness present in the spiritual world that is comprised of healers, gurus and many others who aren't so vested in the beneficial interest of others.

Dark energy vampires are amongst the worst, and they often will drain the energy sources of those around them and send negative energy into others. They can be dangerous and putrid dark creatures. As a high energy empath, I have encountered a host of negative spiritual people, and usually those people aren't even spiritual at all.

There are a number of those out there including the energy vampires, who have an innate ability to project and to send and receive energy, to negative people who claim to be healers yet practice some form of witchcraft or the dark arts and are usually vested only in money and not much else. Energy vampires are amongst the most dangerous of spiritual people and they have learned how to send and receive energy and are the darkest of beings and will often manipulate energies and are a hugely negative source of energy amongst us. Many energy vampires are mentally Ill and have different forms of schizophrenia. Yet their energetic capabilities are very real and they are able to do anything they desire with energy.

What is an empath? An empath is a person who lives their life by the philosophy of being a moral and good person and a person who can deeply feel other people's emotions and pain. Empath's usually harbor the qualities of being kind, caring people and givers as opposed to the energy vampire that is the total opposite. They are known for being selfish, unapologetic takers and are very greedy and mean people. The empath is in severe danger of extreme and major spiritual crisis if they aren't careful about who they surround themselves with. The empath is someone who is generally targeted by energy vampires due to the fact that they harbor a large amount of free energy and have an abundance of energy while the energy vampire is usually a creature that is lacking in energy or depleted.

Stealing someone's energy and power is a huge deal and not something to be taken lightly. People often mock the concept of energetic vampirism, feel it doesn't exist, think it's folklore or fairy tale when in fact it's something that takes place daily and hourly and every second of any human's existence based upon the interactions they have with one another and with others. Energetic vampirism has even been studied by scientists and there are studies that have been done which measure the amount of energy a person has before and after a psychic attack, or varying attacks of different kinds, and there are methods by which scientists have tested and measured a humans energetic levels based on someone taking their energy or not.

Energetic vampirism is something that is severe in life and society and not something that should be taken lightly. It's something that affects each and every one of us in our daily lives whether we recognize it or not and will always be a manner in which a person's energy or life force will be tampered with in some way and either stolen or even destroyed.

Energetic vampirism is not only a violation of one's personal space, their soul and energy body, it embodies the total destruction of a person's life, their current life, every aspect of their existence and even their future. Energetic vampirism is the complete destruction of a person in many different aspects and facets of their life. It is not just s violation or theft of their energetic space, body or soul though even that is too harrowing to comprehend because invading someone's energy body and soul is a very severe and dangerous thing to do to another human being.

Many people may not understand or even believe in the concept of energy vampirism, but it is something that takes place every second of the day and happens to every human on the planet and to many animals. Energetic exchanges take place between individuals on a momentary basis, and so do millions of varying forms of energy giving or energy taking. The concept of energetic vampirism is not a paranormal concept that doesn't exist. It comprises every interaction a person has with another individual. The idea of metaphysical energy vampires might be a concept that people may feel is paranormal in nature, however numerous scientific studies have been done to even prove the existence of energetic vampirism or varying energy levels within a human being.

Empaths and spiritual empaths or mediums are amongst those who might unfortunately encounter energy vampire of varying and complex natures and this is because these particular people possess a gift or varying gifts and their energies are not only grand in nature or high, and a large amount, but these particular people hold a receptive psychic sensor within them that is emitting large and bold signals out to the world or to others and their high energy, strong vibes along with their very definite psychic sensors and magnets that are out there are a huge signal to others, negative energy or low energy people and to psychic or energy vampires or others out there who are dark in nature or might even possess dark empathy and are not of the light or who have a level of awareness of the psychic world yet in a dark aspect.

Those involved in the dark arts or who are aware of energy can easily pick up on the large and bold signals being sent out by bold empaths who usually aren't aware this is occurring and worse never developed the practice of protecting themselves and their energy and shielding themselves from these negative predators in some form. You will often find that extremely positive and kind empaths who put their positive energy out there willingly in order to project positivity, will often be a huge target for those who are negative in any form or those who practice any form of negativity or evil.

## Victims of energy vampires

Many victims of energy vampires feel powerless and much less empowered in general in their everyday lives. They feel as if a portion of themselves has been stolen from them and as if they have been consistently depleted or drained. Their energy has been taken from them in large amounts usually, and they feel weak in general. They don't have enough energy to spend on other people or events in their life. Many victims have a host of health issues ranging from anxiety to stress and can become depressed or even suicidal. Many are overwhelmed by stress and may feel on edge most of the time.

## Refuse to move on or accomplish goals

Feel weak or defeated- many people may feel weak or defeated or even feel inferior to others because their energy or life force has been stolen and they don't possess the energetic levels that are normal for them or that can sustain them in a healthy form.

These people can also be revictimized by others because there are gaping holes in their energy body and worse, they are usually depleted to the level of not possessing a healthy life force any longer and are full of negative toxic and trauma energies.

## Feel inferior to others

Many victims of energy vampires may not feel whole or their fully happy healthy selves- they have been energetically depleted in various forms by very disordered or toxic persons or people and are full of other negative emotions such as fear, confusion, vulnerability, trauma

There are gaping holes in someone's energy body and aura- this allows for more victimization to occur and for more negativity to take place within a person's experiences or life, rather than healthy or positive experiences. These holes create issues in a person's aura and energy body, and constantly will prevent a person from being whole and healthy in their energetic body.

This leaves a person energetically vulnerable and prey to a whole host of predators out there who can sense these energetic wounds and will take full advantage of them if given the opportunity or if they're introduced to their presence in some form.

## Are full of negative emotions and trauma energies

Are full of negative emotions such as fear, horror, toxicity, trauma and fear that these experiences will happen again, which in turn will cause that very ideation to occur.

Are full of trauma energies which are just energies that are the result of a dangerous trauma bond that has formed and the victim is usually the one that carries the pathological trauma energy, while the perpetrator may carry their own trauma energy and negative toxic energy but will often steal the healthy energy of the victim and will hold their energy which most people will define as a person's power.

When someone states that a victim's power is being stolen more often than not, unbeknownst to them, they are often talking about a person's life force or energy being stolen from a person in a great and unfortunate format. A person's power is being stolen from them in a major way and it's something that will affect their life in huge ways and waves and can do a significant amount of damage and negativity to one's life.

## Feel weak or dilapidated

Victims of energy vampires feel extremely weak and dilapidated. They have had their energy and life force stolen from them and have a hard time existing and being in their natural state. When an energy vampire takes energy from a victim, it steals their power, strength and life force, leaving them very weak, down and many times even sick or unable to function. Many times, a person who is victimized can't think straight, can't walk right, and overall have a hard time doing things. Energy vampires try to do a lot of damage to their victims and don't want them having an easy life or doing tasks with ease, they want to make things more difficult for them.

## Have gaping holes in Their energy body or aura

Victims of energy vampires are going to have some serious energetic problems in their body and life. When an energy vampire strikes and attacks a victim and takes their energy, they actually do so by focusing on a certain area of their energy body, and then suctioning or taking energy from that very area and throughout their entire energy body. This leads to holes in a person's energy body and their aura.

## Have a Hard Time Functioning

Those who are victims of vampires have a very hard time functioning for their energetic life force has been depleted and they have been deemed to be made weaker by the vampire, and as a result have a harder time being able to function like a normal person would. They often feel weak, lack internal strength, and have a host of energetic issues.

## Need to have their chakras realigned

People who've undergone vampire attacks are in serious need of having their energy centers healed and their chakras realigned. What does this mean? It just means that they will need their chakras healed and realigned in some format only because the energy vampire does severe damage to a person's energy centers and energetic body.

# Chapter 2

# CHARACTERISTICS OF ENERGY VAMPIRES

People are at different and varying energy levels from each other. Everyone is at their own special level of energy and those with similar energies tend to congregate and be together. Those with higher energies generally will be around or associate with people of a similar energetic level. However, there are people whose energy is at a better wavelength or frequency and that is because those particular people haven't experienced what someone else may have experienced namely someone who may have encountered any form of abuse.

There are many varying characteristics present within an energy vampire. These are not happy, healthy, normal, or sane people that function on a normal day-to-day basis like most humans do. Energy vampires function in a mode where they are constantly depleted of energy, and are in constant need of regaining their own energetic self by taking or stealing energy from others.

Energy vampires often ask you to repeat yourself multiple times so they can take your energy this way. It's a sad and pathetic attempt at making you feel insignificant and leeching your life force. This is just one of many tactics they often use. They generally use a variety of techniques to take a person's life force, all of which are strange and pitiful and show their lack of class amongst other poor qualities they tend to possess.

They often attempt to make you feel inferior or insignificant or lesser than them in some form in order to steal bits of your life force or large portions of it.

It's imperative to stop interacting with an energy vampire or anyone who takes your energy power or life force- they will often continue this pattern and just will not stop. Whatever category they're in, they will often continue this spiritual abuse and will never have healthy or positive interactions with you.

I can often spot out an energy vampire right away. I can get a strong sense of someone's energy and what they're capable of. Most people aren't energy vampires but have the capability to take someone's energy due to being evil or ignorant- anyone can do it really. It doesn't take any special skills to take another person's energy or life force- it simply takes an ignorance that is unheard of, stupidity, possessing low toxic and negative energy, and the desire to do evil and just steal something of someone that doesn't belong to a person.

Most energy vampires have lost their ability to produce positive and good energy, and are full of low and dark energies which are painful and difficult to have within them. When they encounter people with positive energies, they get really excited and giddy and it's because they are getting ready to take their energy and get excited by feeling this very energy. Most are extremely arrogant and are either narcissists, abusers, sociopaths, or a combination of the above. Some aren't those things but just possess an arrogance that is unheard of. Some or many of these people have often delved in the dark arts in some form and may be under the influence of other things.

## Characteristics of energy vampires:
## Low energy

These people possess a low amount of energy and it's something you can sense. They are usually full of darkness, anger, hate and the negative or fear-based emotions. Teenagers can sometimes possess low energies or energies full of dysfunction or low development and that's because they are young people developing into adults, and haven't come into their full energetic selves yet.

Whereas children are usually full of positive pure energies, teenagers are full of energies that could be negative or toxic in nature, are at varied or in primitive states of energetic or emotional development, and might harbor negative feelings or emotions as a result of their current development state or as a result of their home or school life, surroundings, environment, parental upbringing etc. There are many adults and people who are of low energy.

## Dark energy

People having dark energy around them, within them, or just as some part of them. This is something you can generally sense or read or notice about someone. Energy vampires are often full of dark energy and negative forces. They are full of the dark emotions and anger and are often angry, mean, condescending, belittling people and rarely harbor positivity or good or decent emotions in them.

## Loud or bold

They will often be very loud or bold around someone they want to victimize- because this is a way they can take someone's energy or life force.

### Arrogant narcissistic or angry

Many energy vampires are incredibly arrogant, angry, or narcissistic and are not happy people within themselves or internally. On top of having less internal energy, their life forces have become compromised themselves and they have lesser than decent qualities present. They are angry, bitter, miserable and unhappy people in general and live their lives stealing and taking from others and are not good or decent people.

### Rude or belittling condescending

Many people who practice vampirism are rude or belittling and very condescending towards others. They enjoy putting people down and making them feel lesser than they are and can be rude people in general.

### Intrusion of someone's personal space

They often intrude in people's personal spaces, and they do this because it is one way they can take someone's energy. People's energies radiate outwards, and many energy vampires will step into someone's personal space in order to steal and take energy for themselves.

# Gets someone to trust them

Psychic vampires are all around us. They come in many different forms from a random negative energy vampire to a person that can actually take someone's energy very willingly using their metaphysical or psychic supernatural abilities. There are many kinds of psychic vampires that exist in society. What is an energy vampire? An energy vampire or energetic vampirism is the negative aspect of taking someone's energy willingly or sometimes unconsciously, without the other person's permission or knowledge.

Energy vampires are all around us and they are everywhere. Energy vampirism is something that some people are aware of, but that the general population really has no knowledge of or has thought about or thinks about on a regular basis. Most people aren't introduced to this negative aspect or these types of interactions that take place on a regular basis anyway or have little knowledge of this. The reason for this is because these people aren't empaths or don't have a large amount of energy around them, just floating them or in space for others to notice or take. In other words, these people simply aren't high energy beings or possess a certain amount of positive energy, than those who do may experience as a result of this.

The others who experience energy vampirism regularly tend to be those who are victimized or abused by abusers, narcissists, psychopaths, sociopaths or that nature of person. The abused or those who are victimized tend to be the ones who become aware of the aspects of energy vampirism and the taking of one's life force by experiencing it themselves through extreme circumstances of abuse, mistreatment or varying complex forms of this.

Empaths and spiritual empaths or mediums are amongst those who might unfortunately encounter energy vampire of varying and complex natures and this is because these particular people possess a gift or varying gifts and their energies are not only grand in nature or high, and a large amount, but these particular people hold a receptive psychic sensor within them that is emitting large and bold signals out to the world or to others and their high energy, strong vibes along with their very definite psychic sensors and magnets that are out there are a huge signal to others, negative energy or low energy people and to psychic or energy vampires or others out there who are dark in nature or might even possess dark empathy and are not of the light or who have a level of awareness of the psychic world yet in a dark aspect.

Those involved in the dark arts or who are aware of energy can easily pick up on the large and bold signals being sent out by bold empaths who usually aren't aware this is occurring and worse never developed the practice of protecting themselves and their energy and shielding themselves from these negative predators in some form. You will often find that extremely positive and kind empaths who put their positive energy out there willingly in order to project positivity, will often be a huge target for those who are negative in any form or those who practice any form of negativity or evil.

## What the energy vampire often does with the energy.

The narcissist will often try to use it to make themselves happy or try to emulate how the victim used to feel, after witnessing their behaviors and reactions.

They also use it to give to others and will be very positive and friendly to others and seek to steal that energy and give it to others- projecting and displaying that positivity and happiness that the empath or victim deserves towards others, not the victim who deserves it.

They use it to feel energetically superior to the victim and superior and to make the victim weak or inferior. It's a high or power trip for them as well.

The abuser will just hold and use it for themselves because really they just wanted to steal it from the super positive gifted soul, and wanted that person to have less of it or wanted them to suffer in some way.

They too hold some form of a power trip over the victim by holding their energy, and they also prevent the energy from leaving them by being very irrationally negative to the victim and you'll find that happening often. They have no desire to project any form of positivity towards the victim and they do so all with purposeful intent.

The metaphysical energy vampire usually manipulates the energy in various forms, intermingling it with their own sick dark energies and uses it for all kinds of dark things.

They also use the energy for all kinds of various purposes using their abilities and it's not in a positive way- it's in a dark intrusive and evil way.

They often dump dark energy back into the victim, and create a mechanism by which they do this as an energetic device or siphon and it is very painful and malicious.

I despise energy vampires. They get giddy if they're around you and begin giggling and asking you to repeat yourself or will make condescending statements towards you and try to put you down in some form.

Most energy vampires are extremely bitter nasty people and commit their acts intentionally. The second they realize someone's energy is there or there is a positive person around they will do what they can to leech or steal their energy. They put on a good show of pretending to act friendly or positive, but the host or victim will constantly get drained abused mistreated energetically or spiritually and the energy vampire just won't stop.

These are extremely toxic and dysfunctional people and if you're their victim, you can sense and know this right away. There are painful and dark energetic exchanges that take place and can be frightening in nature. I worked in sales and in one particular sector I dealt with large groups of toxic energy vampires. Most people I spoke with were extremely negative hostile and strove to take my energy. They were very fake people putting on a facade or were just openly hostile. I had worked in sales for decades, but I've never encountered this level of nasty vampirism in my life.

Many people can be dangerous and toxic energy vampires and are some of the worst kinds you can find. They will very intricately take one's energy and do so with nothing but malice and hatred. I did not find this type of clientele in any sales field, only the horrors of a specific field, which were full of very toxic energy vampires. They were usually very bitter, negative in nature, and even if they aren't low on energy they would literally try to destroy people or take their energy in the most toxic and hostile way possible. I had people constantly saying they couldn't hear me, forcing me to repeat myself dozens of times even though they understood me, act as if I wasn't speaking clearly, insult or put me down, harass or yell at me and do anything in their power to be negative abusive mean cruel etc.

# Chapter 3

## TYPES OF ENERGY VAMPIRES

There are many different types of energy vampires out there. It is not easy to pinpoint them, and they all generally hold the same values and seek to steal and bring down their victims and ruin their energy body and do what they can to take for themselves from a person. We must protect ourselves from energy vampires and from their treasonous acts upon a person. By knowing the different types that exist out there we can learn to recognize them and be able to gain and develop greater protection from them.

Energy vampires can be people who take energy simply by interacting with a person, being dramatic, throwing fits and by acting in other erratic or irrational ways, using guilt, fear, by demanding attention or they can be energy vampires who possess supernatural abilities and have the ability to manipulate energies and can easily steal energy through their own energetic abilities.

Energy vampires generally fall into two categories- natural and unnatural energy vampire.

## Natural Energy Vampire

A natural energy vampire harbors a natural gift or possesses supernatural, otherworldly energetic abilities that they are usually born with. They often do this through their own gifts or abilities and possess the ability of dark empathy which is a very negative form of empathy where they're able to feel and understand people's emotions and needs and use this ability for their own negative reasons. They do this intentionally and seek to manipulate or exploit or manipulate others for their own emotional energy or life force. Unlike unnatural energy vampires, they may be more aware of their impact on others and use this to gain power or control.

## Unnatural Energy Vampire

The unnatural energy vampire doesn't generally possess natural or gifted capabilities of dark empathy or energetic theft but does so through other unnatural means such as exploiting people through negativity, constant need for attention, or by being overtly demanding. Some do this intentionally and others do this unintentionally. They use tactics such as guilt, fear or emotional blackmail to gain what they want out of a person and to steal and take someone's life force or energy.

There are varying types of energy vampires, and they all cause damaging effects on their victims and possess traits specific to them to be able to effectively take energy from others.

## The conscious energy vampire

The conscious energy vampire gains energy by consciously taking it from others willingly and with ill intent to steal someone's life force or power, and doesn't care about the damage or harm they cause them. They do it all on purpose and with intent to cause harm to their victim and take their life-force from them.

## The unconscious energy vampire

There are energy vampires who sometimes unconsciously take people's energy. They are not always aware they are doing this and have a natural knack to make this happen. These people generally have negative empathic energetic abilities and are able to take energy on their own and do so unconsciously and still wreak a lot of havoc on a person and on their energy body. They also can unconsciously take energy by throwing fits, raging, or throwing a tantrum and can do so without their natural energetic means.

## The abuser who takes energy

The abuser who takes energy is just a general abuser who might be abusive in any given social setting, a domestic violence abuser, or any type of this personality who generally takes energy through their abusive and negative actions towards a victim. Abusers who take energy can be predatory towards their victims and can be unnatural energy vampires which are those who take energy by non-energetic means, or natural energy vampires those who take energy through energetic and supernatural means which a person is naturally gifted with.

## The narcissist who takes energy

The narcissist is an energy vampire who is a natural one and one who takes means through narcissistic tendencies. They are people with NPD or narcissistic personality disorder and are very negative and hostile in nature. A person will want to avoid this type of energy vampire completely as they use their natural gifts and abilities to destroy, hurt or ruin a person and to steal their life-force as well using narcissistic abuse and evil.

### The rude random stranger who takes energy

Sometimes, people come across strangers who are incredibly rude to them and behave in a specific way towards them. Many times, these kinds of people are energy vampires in disguise, and they often are attempting to take an unsuspecting person's energy by being very rude, getting in someone's personal space, or intruding in that person's life in some format. It's important to learn how to identify this kind of person so that you can effectively avoid them if they attempt to start being negative towards you or in your life.

### The significant other who takes energy

Many times, people's spouses are major energy vampires in a person's life and a spouse knows their partner best and knows exactly what to say and how to take a person's energy naturally and unnaturally. It is imperative that a person identify when their spouse is taking their energy because it can have devastating and harrowing effects on a person's life, space, mental health and their physical health as well.

### The family member who takes energy

There are many family members in a person's life who can be energy vampires. Family members can be very vindictive and evil towards someone and end up taking a family member's energy and a person needs to learn how to spot out who in their immediate family is an energy vampire and the tactics they may be using to take their energy.

## The friend who steals energy

There are people who are someone's close confidante and friend who actually engage in this egregious behavior of taking and stealing a person's life force. It's important to learn how to identify who is taking a person's energy especially if it is a friend and to stop this behavior from happening.

## The metaphysical predatory energy vampire

The metaphysical energy vampire is one of the most dangerous types for they take energy through their own metaphysical gifts and natural energies and can be a huge hazard for anyone if they are a target. They have a supernatural ability to manipulate energy and can easily steal it from someone without even resorting to negative tactics, and a person will need to learn effective techniques in order to remove this type of energy taker from their life.

Now these people can fall into several different categories.

## The narcissistic energy vampire

The narcissistic energy vampire is a person who is a narcissist or has narcissistic personality disorder and who displays acts of vampirism on a person using narcissistic tendencies or characteristics which can be very painful and dangerous for a victim. These include acts of projection, projective identification and raging.

## The sociopathic predatory energy vampire

The sociopathic predator energy vampire is an energy vampire who is a basic sociopath and behaves in the manner that a sociopath does which includes glib shallowness, fakeness, lack of empathy, manipulative behavior, a disregard for the rights of others and other negative qualities. They have difficulty forming genuine relationships and often engage in deceitful or aggressive behavior.

Every energy vampire usually falls into the category of rude, abusive, angry, or hostile but the metaphysical energy vampire is generally a narcissist or a dangerous sociopath and though you don't want to encounter or deal with any of these types of predators, the metaphysical energy vampire is the one you'd least likely want to encounter since they have a negativity that can't be described and they have metaphysical abilities which they use against anyone or their targets especially which are dangerous scary and detrimental to one's life and health.

These energy vampires usually have an awareness and a natural ability they've had most of their lives. Sometimes it's something they've learned but usually it's an ability they have honed or further developed and generally in a negative dangerous or destructive way. Energy vampires typically have low energy or have delved in other art forms where their energy has been taken from them or they've used or depleted it in some form. As a result, they will negatively and intrusively take energy from those around them, other people places or objects but namely from other people.

Normal people take or gain energy in a positive way. This might be from positive social interactions with others, music, movies, concerts, parties, events, social gatherings etc. most people aren't aware they are gaining positive energy from these things or aren't focused on getting positive energy- they simply are living their life and enjoying life the best they can or experiencing it. Many people gain good or positive energy from the beach, nature, the sun etc. Energy vampires have a different outlook on experiences, life, or events. While they may gain energy from nature or other aspects in the physical and material world, they are also seeking to thrive and gain energy off other humans as hosts and will prey upon varying people in order to gain a human's energy or life force.

Usually if they're taking energy from other objects or nature it's done in a negative context or by means of the dark arts, negativity, witchcraft, etc. This is how they continue the cycle of evil they live breathe and perpetuate and why they are just full of instability, evil, darkness and have an erratic sick nature. They also can't properly create or maintain good energy or their own energies, so they are constantly taking energies from other people, and they never get enough supply.

The high energy positive empath will often be huge target for these predators because these people possess a large abundance of good and positive light energy, and these people will easily feed off them in all kinds of ways. Their energy is also usually very pure, full of love and light, and may come directly from the higher dimensions. They even create an energetic mechanism by which they will take a person's good energy and dump negative energy into that person. This can have a huge negative impact on someone's life and if someone's finds themselves to be a target of a metaphysical energy vampire, they may find negative things or events happening in their life at a rapid pace. An energy vampire can not only wreak havoc with a person's life but can change the course of someone life with their evil behaviors and create an endless amount of chaos intentionally.

The narcissistic energy vampire is generally just a narcissist with their personality disorder, and a person who chooses to steal a victims life force in the most dangerous devastating and drastic ways possible. A narcissistic energy vampire will never help out or support their victim. They will make sure the victim is at a lower energy level than theirs and will work and fight to constantly take their energy. They can't handle the victim being happy and being excited or themselves most of the time- they want to bring the victim down and make sure they are upset, angry, depressed, down, suffering or hopeless. They often want to be above their victim and even so energetically and will use various tactics to take their energies.

What is the motive of the energy vampire? Well, each type of energy vampire may or may not have different motives, but they all have different ideations or reasons for why they are leeching the life force and energy of a person.

The narcissistic energy vampire- their motive is to destroy the life of the victim ultimately and currently and in very creative ways. The narcissistic energy vampire seeks to weaken their victim, make sure they are energetically low, suffering and depleted. They want their victims to suffer in any form possible. They seek to destroy every element of a victim's life and draining them of their power or energy is only one way they abuse their evil actions on a victim, along with verbal, emotional and other forms of abuse. The narcissistic energy vampire wants the victim to remain a victim and never be confident and to always be in a lower state of energy than they were meant to be.

The metaphysical energy vampire has similar motives, but they really just viciously, arrogantly and in the most evil form possible just seek to steal a hosts life force or energy because they are low on energy or it has become a habit or their lifestyle and they have a need or desire to take someone's energy and deplete them. They may feed off a victim a few times or they may do so long term and multiple or hundreds of times. They usually create a direct connection to the victim and feed off them constantly or regularly and this can become a very dangerous and terrifying situation for the victim.

The empath is in the most danger of becoming a victim of any energy vampire but especially a metaphysical predatory vampire because they are full of positive, divine, and light energy and great feel-good energy that which the negative dark energy vampire just doesn't possess. They are often connected to the divine, source and even universal energies are surrounding and aiding them in their life and mission and the dark negative nasty energy vampire will feed off them in the most evil way possible. They may even steal their divine connections to source or snuff out their energy and life force. The metaphysical energy vampire is an extremely dark creation and will stop at no end to do evil to a good decent good-hearted empath who has no ill intention towards them. The metaphysical dark energy vampire will often steal all of their good life forces and energies and even fill the empath with dark and disturbing frightening energies. There are no bounds that the dark metaphysical energy vampire will surpass when it comes to their interactions with an empath.

An empath can generally sense who might be taking their energy. Energy vampires can easily feed off someone with their knowledge, but most of the time they may mention to the victim what is happening at some point, and even if they don't, an empath is generally keen to identifying who might be involved in the energetic interactions they are feeling that are going on within them.

I have dealt with many forms and types of energy vampires and have experienced the manner in which many will steal the life force of a victim. I can usually handle the energetic vampirism because it might just be one metaphysical vampire doing it as opposed to many. Prior to writing this book, I had a spiritual crisis going on, whereas I was having to deal with multiple vampires that had encountered my presence and who were victimizing me in different forms. This can be a very frightening, painful, and challenging ordeal as there are multiple vampires attacking a person at once and even fighting for a person's energy and to dominate them in some form.

# Chapter 4

# The Empath and the Energy Vampire

## The interactions between empath and energy vampire

Energy vampires love to take the energy of the spiritual empath simply because they have so much energy to take.

Spiritual empaths are harbingers of positive energy. They have a natural connection to higher energies, dimensions, realms, and to the heavens and upper realms.

Many people do as well yet don't really know this but empaths have a special and pure connection as well as being trained in the spiritual arts or having a connection to their spirit guides, angels, ascended masters and other spiritual guides or masters of this nature that are present in the universe.

Energy vampires do not possess this connection and even if they do, they fail to recognize it or care. They are usually connected to dark energies, dark entities and take advantage of the dark arts, and use their energy to harvest more negative or painful dark energy, rather than turning to the light and attempting to be a part of it. They would rather take energy from positive energy or high energy positive people, rather than creating their own positive energy and using it for themselves.

Empaths are often at the most risk of becoming targets of energy vampires due to the energies they possess and the fact that they are beacons of light and possess an abundance of positive energies and have energies that are flamboyant and project outwards very strongly. Empaths are very high energy people and they and most high energy people are at risk of becoming targets of energy vampires. People with low energies are not targeted by the energy vampire as they are not able to take energy from those who do not possess it of course, and high energy people especially empaths possess a very pure positive light energy that energy vampires seek to obtain. Energy vampires can often easily sense the energies of empaths and will gladly take advantage of them and use the empath's energy for themselves without a care as to how it affects, hurts or damages the person.

It angers me greatly when a lower class creation such as an energy vampire so callously takes my energy in the most painful and intrusive pointless ways simply because as a result of this I'm not only unable to function, but empaths and specific kinds of people have goals in life and they need their energy to enhance their mission and goals and they have a desire and often use their energies to raise the vibration of others of the planet, even unconsciously and this is a natural process that is taking place every second of a person's existence.

Empaths have a higher purpose and many are light workers who are on this planet to do and spread the concept of good or love and light and positivity, and there are very negative and dark monsters there not only lurking but stealing the very beautiful, special energies of these gifted wonderful people and using this to do nothing, make themselves feel good, stop a light worker from doing their diligent duty on this planet, thwarting their spiritual and life growth, stunting their development, and using their beautiful special energies to do evil and dark deeds that which they partake in using the dark arts or further enhancing their sad dark motives on this planet.

Empaths are gifted with a very special, unique powerful and beautiful energy that is often connected to the divine and to the higher dimensions or even to heaven. The dark energy vampires are connected to evil, the lower realms, dark beings and dark dimensions and they thrive on existing in this frightening and dark form.

Most negative energy vampires that encounter the high divine energy that an empath has, react by displaying a giddy reaction towards this energy and that giddiness is a dangerous warning of the energetic stealing that is going to take place between the individuals. Yes, some other people might get giddy towards an empath's energetic presence, but they do so with good intent and happiness while feeling or sensing their energy.

Most empaths can sense or know who is laughing or giggling in a friendly normal way, and who is doing so with the intent of stealing that very energy of the person. Many disturbed thieves will even carelessly take the empaths energy or a large portion of it and get excited afterwards or display a false sense of happiness because they know possess that person's energy and are giddy with excitement that they're feeling that happiness and goodness. It is an extremely unfair situation for the confused good natured empath who had no idea this level of vampirism was even going to take place.

They slowly create a negative energetic connection by being negative slowly and injecting negativity into a person through conversation and then taking it to other levels, thus creating a siphon or connection.

They pretend to be harmless at first and normal but will slowly use tactics and techniques to take a person's energy.

They get far too close to a person and invade their personal space in an obvious negative way. It's very simple to just steal someone's energy by being in their space in a not so normal manner. They even hold their hands out in someone's personal space with the intent to take their energy.

They use these techniques for a while in order to create a connection with the victim.

They react with bizarre behaviors if a person's energy is somehow going back to them. They will do strange painful or negative behaviors and that's because it allows them to keep or hold onto the energy rather than allowing it to go back to the rightful owner.

If you are an empath, you'll often find yourself at the other end of the spectrum when it comes to your energy being stolen from you and you'll find it happening very often and you'll experience negative people aggressively attempting to or successfully taking your energy with no repercussions. That's because an empath has a large amount of positive amazing energy, and they are often connected to higher or other divine realms and hold or carry the energy of those sacred places.

Most humans are not at the energetic levels or vibrations that an empath are at and most are unable to handle the energies that surround rude people. As an empath you'll often find others unable to handle your presence and you'll get an array of reactions from others towards the energies and vibrations surrounding you or emitting from yourself. That is because many empaths are in a constant state of channeling or are even connected to other higher dimensions and are channeling and emitting those wonderful energies around them.

Empaths are extremely positive good people who are harbingers of good and positive energies. they seek to help and heal others and do their best to bring peace and harmony wherever they are at. Empaths are the opposite of energy vampires, and many energy vampires have a secret and open dislike and even hatred for empaths. Empaths and energy vampires perform a fine dance together as one is a beacon of positivity, while the other is one of negativity hatred and darkness.

The psychic vampire seeks to steal from the higher energy empath, while the higher energy empath seeks to do good and to heal and to help others. They both encounter each other as dual opposites who can't co-exist with each other due to the ill nature of the energy vampire. The energy vampire will do anything it can to bring down, hurt, ruin or even destroy the empath, while the empath will do anything in his or her power to heal and help the energy vampire. Protecting yourself from the targets of the energy vampire is something you'll learn to know and learn in order to be able to thwart its attacks and bad intentions.

Empaths are typically energy givers and they're usually so full of love and an abundance of positive energy that they live without great restrictions and are constantly giving energy and love to others. They feel others are just like them when this isn't the case. Others might be positive and seem friendly, but their energetic interactions are very different from that of an empath. They aren't unconsciously doing light work and sending out huge positive vibes to others without even really being aware of it, but an empath usually is. There are other forces working with an empath to employ these beneficial energetic exchanges going on. Many empaths are healing others energetically unconsciously and there are usually other positive forces at work employing and manifesting these interesting interactions.

As an empath, you must guard your energy and not be so free with others and give your energy to others. It's extremely difficult because it's just a part of an empaths make-up and their energetic lives and cycles. You're constantly producing positive energy and employing it in different ways. To be around a positive empath is an amazing blessing and an experience. Not everyone can handle this experience though.

The negative humans, narcissists, and energy vampires will notice this exchange taking place, and rather than enjoying the positive energy they are experiencing, they get a taste of it and want more and more of it or even want it all. They literally are so self-serving and wicked that they seek and yearn to steal all of the empaths amazing, beautiful energy and take it for themselves. Their ignorance and sickness is very strange and makes little sense. The irony is that the empath is even giving this energy out to them but that's not enough for them. They have no interest in taking a little bit of energy or even sharing the empaths energy with them. They will just go ahead and do what they can to take the energy from the empath themselves. They harbor a seething deep unjustified hatred for the empath, along with a jealousy that this person possesses this energy, and they will ruthlessly begin to employ tactics to take it from the person.

# Chapter 5

# Symptoms of Energetic Vampirism

Energy is the vital source that is the life force of every living creature. Every living being possesses their own unique and personal energy within their souls and energy bodies and it is this energy that sustains them in hundreds of different forms from their nutrition and lifestyle habits, to their job and work, to their workout habits, and interactions with others and every second of living. It affects their mood, their happiness and every person is equipped to be able to deal with their own personal energy. Every person has their own personal energetic signature. No living being has the right to steal or take or interfere with another person's personal space or energy. To do so is a grave evil and sickness and wrong and worse, the effects it can have on the victim are severe and extreme in nature. The energy vampire doesn't care about these things. They don't care about how a victim feels, how their behavior is affecting another person. Their sole interest is to create these very feelings, and they possess this sick evil intent and a notion of sheer carelessness for their very actions.

Every creature has their very own unique energy and their very own personal energetic signature. This is a person's life force that is vital for them to have in order to function, exist and even survive. The arrogance an energy vampire possesses is too disturbing to describe. They feel they have carte blanche to do what they want to unsuspecting victims and they could care less! Many energy vampires may even hold a deep-rooted and seething jealousy for the victims they take advantage of depending on the situation. They may simply feed off random people with the intent to steal their energies or life force, or they may intentionally and using a connection between a victim, feed off them in a more personal and dark format by doing so in a continuous manner for a long period of time with the intent to just continuously victimize them and make sure their life force is being taken from them constantly and that their lives are affected significantly by this.

There are hundreds of symptoms of energetic vampirism that a person can experience or undergo. Energy vampires seek to function solely to steal the life force of others and will do so by any means. Their actions and behaviors can create a horrible host of symptoms in a person that causes severe mental and physical issues and can create and even potentially cause disease to take place in the body, and simply causes serious problems for a person in their life.

## Symptoms of energetic vampirism

Negativity in one's life
Dark energy inside them or their aura
Different forms of hunger
Feeling weak or dizzy
Feeling dark or negative
Feeling energetically depleted
Unable to generate more energy
The feeling that your energy or life force is gone
Not feeling your usual self
Feeling negative or angry
Feeling hatred or other negative feelings
Losing your sense of calm or peace

The other person seeming happy and suddenly energized or excited.

The vampire resorting to more tactics in order to take your energy.

The vampire turning hostile towards you and choosing not to be kind or positive anymore for some reason.

The vampire behaving erratically or strangely- making loud noises or trying to use different tactics to make you feel uncomfortable or saying negative things to you.

The reason for this is people who steal other people's energy and who have a large level of awareness or even some will intentionally behave very negatively towards the victims- that's to make sure that they never return the positive energy or energy they stole and to keep that energy for themselves or contain it within their energy body or keep it for themselves. It's something witnessed from personal experience and seemed very strange, but these people will go on a hostile tirade to remain as negative as possible towards the victim, making sure they keep this energy that isn't theirs and create a void pain and hell for the victim whose energy they stole.

There is also a technique that some energy vampires use and that is they will slowly and viciously try to start off by injecting negativity into someone's life and through their conversations. They start off by taking energy this way and then they escalate the abuse by inserting more negative energy into the situation.

# How Energy Vampires Function

Energy vampires function solely to steal the life force of others and through the notion and natures of selfishness and rarely harbor the concept of being selfless or wanting to give to others. they are harsh and abrasive takers and will do anything to take from others and become very toxic when it comes to their natures and in their dealings with people.

The reason these people are called vampires is because they are sucking the energy out of others the same way vampires are known to suck out of people or victims.

We are energetic beings who exist in this realm, and it is a great part of us that never ceases to halt us or become a part of our beings or souls. Energy is a vital part of our lives, souls, our exchanges with others and every aspect of our lives.

The energy vampire is an extremely dark devious selfish arrogant and vicious monster that feels it can help itself to a person's energy without any care or consequences towards the victim or what they may be doing to someone's life, their body soul energy etc. Most of the time, with their behaviors come the extreme intent to harm callously a person in varying forms and even worse, the desire to destroy a person's very life force and energetic power. It is a cruel form of evil that these predators possess, and they have no desire to admit to their behaviors or change them at all. They believe they are entitled to doing what they want and to a person's energy.

## How to identify an energy vampire

## Feeling drained or exhausted after spending time with them

People often feel very exhausted and drained after spending time with an energy vampire. They feel many different emotions and aren't doing too well after encountering them. They feel their energy being taken from them and just feel weak in general.

## Constantly listening to their problems without them reciprocating

Many energy vampires may use tactics such as constantly complaining about their life or their problems and rarely reciprocate or ask about another person's life or situation. They are always talking about themselves as if they are the most important people on the planet and as if no one else matters. They are very selfish and seek to serve their needs only.

## Feeling like they always demand attention or validation

Energy takers are in constant need of attention or validation from others. They may constantly talk about themselves or even fish for compliments or validation. While they are using these techniques, they are stealing the energy of another person or sucking the life out of them.

## Constant complaining or being negative

Negative energy vampires are usually constantly complaining or being negative about things. By utilizing the concept of negativity, they can generally effectively take energy from others. This is a tactic that many use in order to take people's vital life-force.

## Not respecting your boundaries

Energy vampires rarely respect a person's boundaries. If you object to the behaviors they are displaying and ask them to stop or to respect your boundaries, they will always almost ignore your requests or wishes and continue with their disrespectful and indecent actions and behaviors. They rarely to never respect the boundaries of others and impede upon them.

## Throwing a fit over any given thing that occurs

People are at different and varying energy levels from each other. Everyone is at their own special level of energy and those with similar energies tend to congregate and be together. Those with higher energies generally will be around or associate with people of a similar energetic level. However, there are people whose energy is at a better wavelength or frequency and that is because those particular people haven't experienced let's say what someone else may have experienced namely someone who may have encountered any form of abuse.

Energy vampires often ask you to repeat yourself multiple times so they can take your energy this way. It's a sad and pathetic attempt at making you feel insignificant and leeching your life force. This is just one of many tactics they often use. They generally use a variety of techniques to take a person's life force, all of which are strange and pitiful and show their lack of class amongst other poor qualities they tend to possess.

They often attempt to make you feel inferior or insignificant or lesser than them in some form in order to steal bits of your life force or large portions of it.

Stop interacting with an energy vampire or anyone who takes your energy power or life force- they will often continue this pattern and just will not stop. Whatever category they're in, they will often continue this spiritual abuse and will never have healthy or positive interactions with you.

I can often spot out an energy vampire right away. I can get a strong sense of someone's energy and what they're capable of. Most people aren't energy vampires but have the capability to take someone's energy due to being evil or ignorant- anyone can do it really. It doesn't take any special skills to take another person's energy or life force- it simply takes an ignorance that is unheard of, stupidity, possessing low toxic and negative energy, and the desire to do evil and just steal something of someone that doesn't belong to a person.

Most energy vampires have lost their ability to produce positive and good energy, and are full of low and dark energies which are painful and difficult to have within them. When they encounter people with positive energies, they get really excited and giddy and it's because they are getting ready to take their energy and get excited by feeling this very energy. Most are extremely arrogant and are either narcissists, abusers, sociopaths, or a combination of the above. Some aren't those things but just possess an arrogance that is unheard of. Some or many of these people have often delved in the dark arts in some form and may be under the influence of other things.

The narcissistic energy vampire is generally just a narcissist with their personality disorder, and a person who chooses to steal a victims life force in the most dangerous devastating and drastic ways possible. A narcissistic energy vampire will never help out or support their victim, they will make sure the victim is at a lower energy level than theirs and will work and fight to constantly take their energy. They can't handle the victim being happy and being excited or themselves most of the time- they want to bring the victim down and make sure they are upset, angry, depressed, down, suffering or hopeless. They often want to be above their victim and even so energetically and will use various tactics to take their energies.

What is the motive of the energy vampire? Well, each type of energy vampire may or may not have different motives, but they all have different ideations or reasons for why they are leeching the life force and energy of a person.

An empath can generally sense who might be taking their energy. Energy vampires can easily feed off someone with their knowledge, but most of the time they may mention to the victim what is happening at some point, and even if they don't, an empath is generally keen to identifying who might be involved in the energetic interactions they are feeling that are going on within them.

I have dealt with many forms and types of energy vampires and have experienced the manner in which many will steal the life force of a victim. I can usually handle the energetic vampirism because it might just be one metaphysical vampire doing it as opposed to many. Prior to writing this book, I had a spiritual crisis going on, whereas I was having to deal with multiple vampires that had encountered my presence and who were victimizing me in different forms.

Empaths are often at the most risk of becoming targets of energy vampires due to the energies they possess and the fact that they are beacons of light and possess an abundance of positive energies and have energies that are flamboyant and project outwards very strongly. Energy vampires can often easily sense the energies of empaths and will gladly take advantage of them and use the empath's energy for themselves without a care as to how it affects, hurts or damages.

# Animals and Energy Vampirism

Most animals aren't energy vampires, though rifts can occur between various creatures and animal's energetic exchanges aren't normally taking place on an intentional level. An animal might bully get angry at or mistreat another animal depending on the given situation and there are energetic exchanges that take place in any form between any living being, but one animal's energy isn't significantly stolen, though their energy can often be affected the same way any human's energy is affected from any form of mistreatment, abuse or bullying. An animal's energy can change significantly and be affected by any form of abuse or bullying done by another animal, and they can project that through their energies the same way a human might. An animal's energetic levels or energy can reflect the kind of abuse or treatment they are receiving or whether or not they have experienced any form of trauma or negativity in their life.

However a human's abuse towards an animal can have harrowing effects on an animal's energy and their emotional state of mind and their very souls. A human has the ability to steal the life force of an animal and there are many who do through extreme evils or abuse. The levels of abuse a human are capable of and commit contain large amounts of damage and atrocities done to the victims and animals are not immune to having their energies upset or affected by the behavior of other humans.

Animals give out an unlimited abundance of love, joy, positive and good energies and they are in desperate need of that energy being given back to them. They also deserve only good and positive energies being given their way as well as extreme love and respect. Animals respect their human companions or fellow planet beings and deserve only respect and kindness in return. Animals do not hold any ill will or intent towards others and though they may commit abuses or might display acts of negativity sometimes towards other animals, they are very pure creatures who are not about conflict or hurting others.

Animals are beautiful loving caring kind beings who usually are full of extreme positivity kindness good and love. Whereas there are instances of bullying or abuse that do occur between animals of all kinds, for the most part they do contain an abundant amount of love, caring, and trust within their souls and beings.

## Energy Vampirism and Spirituality

There are many negative aspects of spirituality that can be present in someone's life. Dark energy or vampirism is something that is common amongst those who practice a negative form of being spiritual. There is a true and defined form of darkness present in the spiritual world that is comprised of healers, gurus, and many others who aren't so vested in the beneficial interest of others.

Dark energy vampires are amongst the worst, and they often will drain the energy sources of those around them and send negative energy into others. They can be dangerous and putrid dark creatures. As a high energy empath, I have encountered a host of negative spiritual people, and usually those people aren't even spiritual at all.

There are a number of those out there including the energy vampires, who have an innate ability to project and to send and receive energy, to negative people who claim to be healers yet practice some form of witchcraft or the dark arts and are usually vested only in money and not much else. Energy vampires are amongst the most dangerous of spiritual people and they have learned how to send and receive energy and are the darkest of beings and will often manipulate energies and are a hugely negative source of energy amongst us. Many energy vampires are mentally ill and have different forms of schizophrenia. Yet their energetic capabilities are very real, and they are very able to do anything they desire with energy.

## Energy vampires and social interaction

Energy vampires often will try to keep talking to you in a particular way to take your energy. It's not a positive beneficial way where they are having a conversation. They will often ask many questions over and over and try to mock you. I worked selling a particular product and noticed that when I dealt with certain people, in the sales positions I had I didn't encounter too many energy vampires.

People enjoyed my good energy and sales abilities and were very friendly and positive.

When I sold a different product though and had to deal with a different clientele, it was a very different story. Almost every customer I dealt with or many of them were hardcore energy vampires. They consistently yelled on the phone, talked very loudly, talked too much yet in a way to be draining, or talked over you, cut you off and got hostile when you attempted to do it back to them.

I remember one day dealing with at least 80 percent of customers being energy takers and finally got this woman on the line. She took my energy, and I attempted to take it back by cutting her off. She got erratic, hostile yelled very loud and continued talking loudly berating me and then hung up abruptly. As a result, most of my energy was taken from me. Most energy vampires know exactly what they are doing and know how to take energy from specific kinds of people especially from high energy empaths.

Energy vampires will get in your space, in your aura, and even do so to absorb your energy. They can be vicious and brutal in their behaviors. There is a way to get your energy back and they get hostile if you attempt to try. You will have to know how to harness energy in some format and use your psychic and mental abilities to somewhat attempt to will it back to you, though it's very difficult.

Energy vampires are brutal unstable and strange people. When encountering most of these people on the phone, I was kind, caring and projected good energy and showed them that. Rather than being nice to me or appreciating my kindness, most clientele of a specific kind acted brutal, hostile, angry, rude, laughed haughtily for no reason, and did anything they could to put me down or take my energy.

# Chapter 6

# How Energy Vampires Take Energy

Those who have this ability innately can easily steal the life force of a person, and they can do other things to a person such as project to them or be in their presence energetically and metaphysically somewhat similar to a ghost around them, can have various forms of energetic sex with them which is having sex with them without being in their physical presence, and can even hurt or physically harm a person using their abilities.

Energy vampires steal the energy of a person by focusing on specific areas of a person or even their chakra points. They then take the energy of a person similar to a suction and will take as much as they can, which creates energetic issues for the host victim. It is a very negative and painful interaction that can leave the victim feeling drained, weak or even sick. It can even create different forms of disease in a person or various health issues. Many energy vampires also create what is considered to be a negative vampiric connection to a host person.

## By throwing fits or starting a fight

Fighting consists of serious energetic exchanges. Once an energy vampire picks a fight with someone, they already have the upper hand in taking someone's energy. They often do so very boldly and viciously in order to destabilize someone's energetic and life force and they'll continue this exchange in order to take more energy and continue this exchange or cycle. They can take energy easier after destabilizing their life force by starting an argument or fight, and then by continuing this through other means of what is involved in an argument in order to take more energy.

## By yelling or being very loud

One way an energy vampire takes energy is by yelling or screaming loud, for this naturally drains a person and takes their life-force. This is one common tactic used by them and the way a person can safeguard themselves from this tactic is to leave the situation immediately once it begins, otherwise their energy and life force will be at risk of being drained or taken from them.

## By talking over someone or interrupting them constantly and then taking over the conversation

Many people can effectively take someone's energy by talking over them constantly, interrupting them or forcing them to repeat themselves. Have you ever been in a conversation where you just can't seem to get a word in? The other person somehow is talking non-stop and making sure that you can't talk? Well, this is a tactic that a person can use intentionally in order to steal a person's energy. Also, if you are talking, an energy vampire can take your energy by making you repeat yourself constantly or even by talking over and then taking over the conversation. These are just a few other tactics they use to steal enormous amounts of energy or life force, and will do so very effectively, arrogantly, and without a care as to how it makes a person feel.

Trying to corner someone in a space or impose on their personal space in various forms.

Energy vampires will often intrude in someone's space to take their energy and do so very arrogantly and feel as if they are entitled to being in a person's space or even taking someone's life force. Most energies are expanding outward in a person's personal space and aura and an energy vampire knows this, so they intrude in a person's space in order to absorb the energy of the other persons. They often do not care about the effects they have in someone's life or the consequences of their actions on someone. Their main goal is to take and steal energy and help themselves to someone's life force and energetic powers and even their personal power.

## By touching people too softly or lightly

Many people who take energy use tactics in order to steal or take energy from someone. They actually touch people too softly or lightly in order to intentionally take energy in some way. If someone often touches you far too lightly, or far too harshly and it happens often and feels unnatural, it is a tactic usually to take a person's energy. This is a common tactic that energy vampires do use to take energy as well that most people do not usually know about.

## By hitting someone or being abrasive or aggressive with them

Energy vampires can often be very abrasive with someone or hit them or get aggressive with them. This is a common tactic to take or steal the energy of another person and they can do so by cornering them aggressively or just being this way in general. It is an effective method to take energy and is something that a person has to resort to recognizing and stopping before the energy vampire can commit this intrusive act on someone.

## By talking extremely long and not getting to the point or stopping

Extreme verbal communication can easily result in major energetic vampire tactics. Most of the time, the person is doing this in order to take someone's energy and their tone or manner in which they speak is very abrasive, negative or not normal. There are people that can talk for a long period of time too who aren't stealing someone's life force or energy. The rule of thumb is, if your energy is being taken- whether intentional or not oe you feel weak or drained, it's being done by a negative draining person or energy vampire.

## By speaking negatively to a person often or constantly or trying to bring them down

Energy takers often speak very negatively to a person or are in a constant state of bringing someone down using negativity, insults and being rude or mean. They often put people down and this is a common tactic or means by which they use to take energy and one method that can actually drain a person's life force.

## By acting hostile towards someone for no reason

Energy vampires often and simply act hostile towards people for no reason. They are not very nice people and resort to acting out, being aggressive and acting hostile in order to destabilize a person's internal life-force and take someone's energy.

Non-energy vampires just do not take energy and with people's intent comes behavior and most of the time, these people have some awareness to what they're doing or why. They might talk nonstop and just end a conversation in order to take someone's energy or life force. Most energy vampires naturally have the ability to take different forms of energy from a person and some learn this ability.

## What the energy vampire often does with the energy

The energy vampire just uses the energy for their own benefit, and once they begin stealing a person's energy they usually just don't stop. Nothing is enough for an energy vampire for once they help themselves to a person, they feel entitled to taking more from that person if they're able to do so. They have no limits, barriers, or morals when it comes to taking energy from innocent and unsuspecting victims and don't give a care as to how a person feels when it comes to symptoms they may experience as a result of being drained or depleted of their life force.

The narcissist energy vampire will often try to use it to make themselves happy or try to emulate how the victim used to feel, after witnessing their behaviors and reactions.

They also use it to give to others and will be very positive and friendly to others and seek to steal that energy and give it to others- projecting and displaying that positivity and happiness that the empath or victim deserves towards others, not the victim who deserves it.

They use it to feel energetically superior to the victim and superior and to make the victim weak or inferior. It's a high or power trip for them as well.

The abuser will just hold and use it for themselves because really they just wanted to steal it from the super positive gifted soul, and wanted that person to have less of it or wanted them to suffer in some way.

They too hold some form of a power trip over the victim by holding their energy, and they also prevent the energy from leaving them by being very irrationally negative to the victim and you'll find that happening often. They have no desire to project any form of positivity towards the victim and they do so all with purposeful intent.

The metaphysical energy vampire usually manipulates the energy in various forms, intermingling it with their own sick dark energies and uses it for all kinds of dark things.

They also use the energy for all kinds of various purposes using their abilities and it's not in a positive way- it's in a dark intrusive and evil way.

They often dump dark energy back into the victim, and create a mechanism by which they do this it's an energetic device or siphon and is very malicious. The energy vampire will often create a harrowing dark scenario where they are siphoning a person's energy and life force, and actually dumping their own negative energy back into that person for the sole reason of stealing their positive energy and making them suffer at the same time.

You need your energy to do great, amazing and powerful positive things and just to live your life. You need it to do light work and good things. It's also yours. They don't need your energy and even if they do it's your energy and they have no right or place to steal or take it at all. But that's not the perspective they hold. They feel they have every right to take it from you and will become belligerent and hostile in order to keep it for themselves. They now believe it is their energy and not yours and you can't convince them otherwise. They aren't going to use it for anything beneficial and they have their own energy.

They might lead you on to extreme degrees or keep you waiting in order to take your energy. Some of these ignorant monsters not only want to take your energy or power and use it for themselves or to benefit or elevate themselves, they just don't want YOU to have your own energy which is hard to grasp or comprehend. The energy of an empath is so enthralling and enticing, energy vampires and negative disturbed people will go to great lengths to keep it away from its owner, and to steal and keep it for themselves.

An empaths energy may be full of extremely beautiful, amazing and positive feelings, thoughts, beliefs, morals, values, sensations. It is warm and comforting and can give anyone eternal happiness and peace. It can give someone intellect and even an abundant amount of knowledge. It is a very valuable unique gift that has been bestowed to this person and others want to take it for themselves. It can allow a person to feel enlightened and give them an abundance of true happiness. The problem is the energy does not belong to this sad vampire and it is not even suited for them. It is given to the empath so they can do beneficial positive things with it and affect others in a beneficial way. The negative sociopathic vampires just use it for nothing or to boost their egos, or to feel good for a while. They are still angry warped creatures inside who are very disordered, and this is their nature.

## How to take your energy back

There is a way to take your energy back if you're able to read and understand energy, or ways to connect back your energy that was stolen from you. It's important to attempt to take your energy back because this is your very life force and only you can really utilize and use it to the best of its nature and worse you need this energy to survive and live. It is part of your body, soul and your very make up. It is definitely not a part of the energy vampires make up. To take your energy back you'll need to cut off contact with the energy vampire in any way you can. This means no verbal communication with them, no written or spoken communication and though most victims are unaware they are targets of a vampire, the ones who are, will need to cut off all ties with this person.

A person can will their energy back through their own energetic abilities, through their mental desires and other means in order to take their energy back. They can also feel the energy being taken from them and since energy is an intangible substance or force, it can be created, recreated or manipulated in some form by those who are able to perceive it, are aware of it or have the capability of being able to manipulate or influence it which can be most people out there.

# Chapter 7

# How To Deal With Energy Vampires

Dealing with an energy vampire is not an easy feat to do. You are attempting to deal with a very negative creature who is a taker and not a giver and someone who seeks to bring you down in some form or just steal your very life force without a care or thought. Energy takers are very persistent in what they choose to do and do not care about the repercussions of their behaviors, or how it makes a victim of theirs feel. The only thing they care about is getting their energetic fix because they have energy issues themselves and are in dire need of energy and have decided rather than creating energy in positive and beneficial ways which they easily can do, they would rather take it from others and create a negative issue and a host of negative symptoms in a person. They have no care or caution towards their actions.

Dealing with an energy vampire is not simple. They are very determined, arrogant, and extreme in their behaviors. Most of the time, a person needs to limit their interaction with one completely and even avoid all contact in order to effectively be able to safeguard their energy and their bodies and lives in general. An energy vampire can have damaging effects not only on a person's energy body and their physical body, but energetic vampirism can have damaging and negative effects in a person's life completely and it's very important to rid yourself of this dangerous person and what they intend to do to you. It takes strategic planning sometimes, and other strategies and methods to handle or deal with one and to eliminate them from your life altogether.

## Signs you could be a victim of energy vampires.

Projecting bold positive energy
A large amount of positive energy
A psychic honing device within yourself
Others being able to sense or pick up on your energy
Others being able to feel your energy or sense how you seem to feel
Inability to handle negativity or aggression
A strong aversion to any form of negativity

A natural love for anything good or positive
An extreme amount of compassion for animals or others.
A love for nature and the world around us
Your presence and energy seem to influence or even bother others
Other people's inability to handle your energy or your presence.
Your energy being stolen, drained or affected by anything negative.

## Ways to protect yourself and your energy

## Shield your energy and your aura

Take courses and learn effective techniques on how to shield your aura and your energy body and how to protect yourself from an energy vampire. Visualize a protective shield around you and your aura and protect yourself with a white light surrounding you and your aura in order to begin protecting yourself from psychic vampire attacks.

## Tone down your energy

If you're energetically capable or aware, figure out tactics on how to tone down your energy so that you aren't projecting as strongly and so an energy vampire can't notice you as easily or take advantage of you

### Stop projecting your positive energy to others

Guard your good vibes and energy. And be very careful with what you project or display around the energy vampire. There are tactics you can use to do this, and you can even learn how to energetically safeguard and protect your energy from one of these kinds of people.

### Limit interaction with the energy vampire

Reduce the time you spend with the person especially in one-on-one situations where their draining behavior and limit your interaction with them.

### Cut off all contact with the energy vampire

It's imperative to have zero interactions with an energy vampire and to cut off all contact with these people. Any interaction you have with them can and will result in your energy or life force being stolen or depleted and you feeling weak, unsure of yourself, dizzy and many other symptoms at hand. Once you cut off all interactions with the vampire you'll be on your way to freedom from this person and the evils they are doing to you.

## Set clear boundaries to limit your interactions

Clearly define what behavior you will or will not tolerate and communicate these boundaries firmly to a vampire. Make sure you stand by these boundaries and never allow the vampire to cross them or throw rages or fits or do things to take your energy or use other communication methods or energetic methods to get what they can out of you. Do not hesitate to say "no" when needed.

## Practice assertive communication

Practicing assertive communication when around or in the presence of an energy vampire can be a great asset to assisting you with communicative techniques to aid and shield yourself against one. Using statements such as "I don't feel comfortable when you focus on negativity or yell at me," or practicing assertive statements and communicating how you feel to an energy vampire can assist you with effectively stopping the techniques they are using against or on you in order to deplete or drain you or affect your life in a negative way.

## Prioritize self-care to replenish your energy

Make time for activities that rejuvenate you and your energy. This includes yoga, spending time in nature, reading, spending time with friends and loved ones, going to the movies, going to a spa, relaxing. It's important to prioritize these activities in your schedule and life to ensure you're recharged. You will need to prioritize extreme amounts of self-care in your life and your routine. This also thwarts a negative energy vampires negative attacks on you because you are fighting an attack and their negativity with different kinds of positive energies.

## Engage in activities that uplift yourself

Engage in activities that uplift yourself or those around you. Focus on positive relationships and make an effort to spend more time with those close to you. Go out shopping, to a movie, spend time at a spa, get a relaxing massage, engage in group behaviors with other people and do what you can to uplift yourself and your life so that the effects of the energy vampire can be thwarted. One method of destabilizing an energy vampire's attacks is by using positive energy in different forms and inundating yourself in positive energy in order to reduce or rid yourself of an energy vampire's negative attacks towards you.

## Seek the support of others

Seek support from positive people as well as surrounding yourself with positive, uplifting individuals who can counteract the effects of energy vampires. If a person is alone, a vampire has more desire and reason to target them, but if a person is surrounded by others, the energy vampire has less desire to target them or feel as if they are an easy target. Energy vampires often target individuals who are by themselves, so always make sure you're never alone with one but that you're surrounded by friends and family on a constant basis.

## Stray from anyone who seems to have dark vibes or dark energy about them

Stay away from low energy or negative people in any form- they will usually try to take your positive energy and do things to you that you can't imagine. They will try to take all of your good positive energy and ruin your life in different ways. They also seek to take it so they can be happy and emulate your happiness. They don't possess happiness of their own.

Dark energy people will seek to steal your positive energy.

People of low energy full of issues depression hate anger will seek to take your energy.

Associate only with positive people who have positive and good vibes energy vampires are easy to spot- guard yourselves from them, never interact with them and keep a strong sense of closure with them.

It's easy to sense and recognize energy vampires. Most people aren't energy vampires or hold the desire to steal someone's energy. Sometimes it can happen accidentally or unconsciously, but that is something that just happens. Energy vampires can easily be recognized because sometimes when they are near you or pass by you, they have a strong energy shield as well though it's usually negative in nature and can affect your energy just by being near you. Usually, they behave in abnormal irrational strange or erratic ways in order to take your energy or life force. It's obvious what they are and what their intent is.

Negative energy vampires aren't only in it to steal a person's energy, most of the time they seek to affect a person's life as well and ruin a person's life with the behaviors they commit. They have no issue rendering someone dysfunctional or affecting their life in the long run on a very negative basis which is very unfair to a victim. For these reasons, it is of extreme importance that a person protects their energies and do whatever they can to escape an energy taker rather than deal with the pain and wrath of one, for their life can be affected in a very negative way by this negative person.

# Chapter 8

# Characteristics of an Empath

Empaths are typically energy givers and they're usually so full of love and an abundance of positive energy that they live without great restrictions and are constantly giving energy and love to others. They feel others are just like them when this isn't the case. Others might be positive and seem friendly, but their energetic interactions are very different from that of an empath. They aren't unconsciously doing light work and sending out huge positive vibes to others without even really being aware of it, but an empath usually is. There are other forces working with an empath to employ these beneficial energetic exchanges going on. Many empaths are actually healing others energetically unconsciously and there are usually other positive forces at work employing manifesting these interesting interactions.

As an empath, you must guard your energy and not be so free with others and give your energy to others. It's extremely difficult because it's just a part of an empaths make up and their energetic lives and cycles. You're constantly producing positive energy and employing it in different ways. To be around a positive empath is an amazing blessing and an experience. Not everyone can handle this experience though.

The negative humans and narcissists and energy vampires will notice this exchange taking place, and rather than enjoying the positive energy they are experiencing, they get a taste of it and want more and more of it or even want it all. They literally are so self-serving and wicked that they seek and yearn to steal all of the empaths amazing beautiful energy and take it for themselves. Their ignorance and sickness is very strange and makes little sense. The irony is that the empath is even giving this energy out to them but that's not enough for them. They have no interest in taking a little bit of energy or even sharing the empaths energy with them. They will just go ahead and do what they can to take the energy from the empath themselves. They harbor a seething deep unjustified hatred for the empath, along with a jealousy that this person possesses this energy and they will ruthlessly begin to employ tactics to take it from The person.

Empaths are highly energetic loving, kind and caring people who are givers of goodness and seek to heal others and be of help and humanity to the planet. There are many different characteristics an empath does possess.

## Empathy

Empaths have a high level of empathy and can understand how others are feeling and in deep and spiritual manners too. Empaths possess empathy in great ways and know how others feel and know what it's like to be in another person's situation and have a great level of understanding, patience and kindness.

## Intuitive and Psychic

Empaths have strong psychic and intuitive skills and seem to know what people are thinking or feeling. Many have the traits of clairsentience, clairaudience, and many other important psychic abilities.

## Compassion

Empaths really have a high level of compassion within them. They are constantly caring for and wanting to help others and do good for others and seek to aid humanity. They have a strong caring heart for those who are down or suffering or in a negative situation and a desire to help people or animals in those situations.

## Sensitive

Empaths are incredibly sensitive people and to the emotions of others and towards their own emotions too. They often need time alone to recharge after social interactions. Because empaths are intuitive, they can sense the emotions of energies of others and are sensitive to all of the feelings that people possess.

## Solitude

Empaths tend to enjoy solitude and focus on their own tasks because if others are around, they tend to focus on others. When alone, empaths tend to refocus and recharge their energies so they can best utilize them for themselves and for the needs of others.

I once dealt with a client who continued giggling throughout our interactions and continuously asked me to repeat myself. She did so with the intent of taking my energy viciously. She would not stop. I've learned that when an energy vampire has a desire to take your energy, you are often at the mercy of their evils, especially if you can't get away from them. She would not stop until I was completely drained, and even after I was drained, she wouldn't stop. Most energy leeches will suck you until you're dry. Being a very positive empath with amazing and beautiful energy I often found myself at the other end of toxic and disturbing energy vampires and negativity sick people.

Many people I encountered didn't think oh boy she has great or wonderful energy- though some did of course. More people than there were vampires weren't vampires and were not toxic in nature. It's just that those who were vampires were extremely dangerous and vicious in their approaches to take my energy. Most of the time they didn't even want my energy- they just sought to make me suffer or bring me down. It was very strange. People can easily share energy, but this is not what happens with the general consensus or populace. You will find very bitter angry negative dark and nasty people who will do what they can to drain you or take your energy.

I have witnessed the extreme levels of energy vampirism based on hundreds of interactions and varying experiences. Rather than these negative people just thinking oh she has good energy or them just being normal towards you, these awful, deranged people will go to excessive and extreme lengths to leech your life force from you. They do anything to bring you down and take your energy from you.

Most energy vampires possess a seething internal negativity within their beings and selves. They seek to destroy and steal the light and good energy from their victims or hosts and are not happy or normal people. People who intentionally victimize others or literally have the intent interest or desire to steal the life force of others generally will possess an internal hatred and evil that is unknown or unheard of to those who do not possess these traits or commit these atrocities, and really just possess an evil and darkness within them that isn't normal behavior and makes little sense.

Even if my energy is stolen by others and I'm low energy or even down or suffering as a result, I still have no desire or want to take anyone else's life force. It is actually a grave evil and sin that many people commit upon others without care and callously, and something that can greatly impact and affect a person's life, life story, current experiences and even their future. Impacts energy vampirism has on a person's life can be great and detrimental.

As an aware energetic empath who is all about positive energy and interactions, I'm extremely aware of interactions between myself and others and also have no interest or desire in taking anyone else's energy. I possess a higher awareness of these concepts and intentionally interact many times with the concept of making sure I'm not taking someone else's energy. I'm extremely careful sometimes when it comes to interactions with others and unfortunately because I do tend to get victimized by negative energy vampires and real ones once in a while, I tend to have a different level of awareness when it comes to energetic interactions.

I don't usually focus on my awareness or behavior and most of the time, people out there are not energy vampires by nature, but there are some diamonds in the rough and rude bad people who tend to be energy vampires and who will attempt to victimize me or others energetically and in other formats in order to make us suffer or steal our life force from us. Just from sole interactions with others and observations I've come to a greater understanding of energy vampires and the methods by which they behave and how they interact with others or techniques they use to take energy form others.

Energetic vampirism can have harrowing and severe effects on a person's life, in their current soul body, their energy body and just their basic interactions with others as well as with life goals and a whole host of arenas. Since there are different kinds of energetic vampirism that exist, each one can have very dangerous and major effects on a person's overall life, their life story and can change the course of someone's life.

## Feel powerless less empowered.

Many people feel disempowered by an energy vampire and feel as if they can't commit to the things they've done or are unable to accomplish their goals, dreams or desires.

Refuse to move on or accomplish goals.

## Feel weak or defeated

Many people may feel weak or defeated or even feel inferior to others because their energy or life force has been stolen and they don't possess the energetic levels that are normal for them or that can sustain them in a healthy form.

These people can also be revictimized by others because they tend to become very weak and have holes in their aura and this can be sensed easily by predators who know exactly what to look for in a victim. Energy vampires taking advantage of a person can end up having devastating long-term effects on a person's life.

## Feel inferior to others

Energetic interactions and energy is an extremely important part of someone's life and a person's life and every living creation's life. People can't live without their life force and energy and the energy that people contain sustains them physically, mentally, emotionally nutritionally and in many other forms. With energy depletion comes a whole host of issues and problems that a person may not face if these things weren't occurring. The energetic life force is the basic nourishment of the inner soul body of s human and should be enhanced, nourished, encouraged to grow using healthy forms, deserves to be in the midst of proper balance and goodness and needs a healthy cultivation in order to assist and support each living being it's a part of.

With energetic dysfunction due to energy vampirism come many different issues in a person or creatures life. You'll often find that people who've been abused or mistreated, have varying and are holding a lower energy level and are full of toxic energies that have been destroyed.

People who are abused will often have a whole host of energetic issues- that's because with abuse comes extreme energetic abuse and dysfunction and is a major reason why abuse victims become stuck in a vicious and unfair cycle of abuse, negativity and trauma- it's because a significant portion of their energy has not only been stolen from them, but the abusers own toxic energy has been intermixed or injected into them by the abuser in some form, and even worse their positive or good energy or their very own life force whatever that may possess isn't whole or healthy any longer- it's depleted, full of negative or toxic energies, full of varying emotions and even turns into trauma energy. An abuse victim is not a healthy whole person any longer because of the nature of energetic abuse that has been done to them and that they've been subjected to.

# Chapter 9

# How To Embrace Your Intuitive Gifts

What are psychic abilities? Psychic abilities are the ability to perceive information beyond the normal human senses such as taste, smell, sound, and include skills like telepathy, clairvoyance, and clairsentience. Many people feel these abilities allow them to gain more insight about events, thoughts, or ideas that aren't really accessible any other way.

In order for a person to develop their psychic abilities, they will need to learn about the different types of abilities and then slowly gain insight into their own abilities and what they're capable of doing. The different types of psychic abilities will be described here and how to activate and learn and develop them. Once a person has learned their own abilities and is able to further them, they will have the means to protect themselves against energy vampires. It's important to have some psychic ability development in order to fight an energy vampire's attacks, their effects and be able to thwart and remove an energy vampire from your life.

Most people do possess intuitive gifts of some sorts. Not everyone might have all of the gifts that are readily accessible, but they can also learn how to tap into them or develop them if they don't possess them. People generally develop their psychic abilities through different practices such as meditation, higher awareness, mindfulness, grounding techniques, and spiritual practice. This can develop spiritual intuition and awareness. Energy work such as reiki or chakra balancing can enhance a person's sensitivity to energy and allow them to become more psychically in tune and develop their personal abilities. Visualization techniques and journaling are also ways a person can develop their personal intuitive abilities.

## How to listen to your psychic Intuition

It's important to listen to your psychic intuition and focus on what your intuition tries to tell you and how it speaks to you in everyday life. Your intuition is an extremely important part of yourself and your energy body as well and your mind and psyche.

Many people don't believe in the concept of psychic intuition or psychic phenomenon, but these concepts are very real and do exist in this world. There are many different types of psychic phenomenon that we need to study and learn the nature of in order to become better protected and higher aware energetic and spiritual beacons who can not only help ourselves but help others as well.

## Clairsentience

Clairsentience is one of the psychic senses, or clairs. Clair means 'clear', while sentience means 'feeling', and clairsentience means 'clear feeling', and is sometimes referred to as 'empathic intuition'. It involves perceiving or sensing information through our emotional or energetic feelings. Clairsentience is the concept of being able to sense things or information through our energetic feelings.

It is the ability to feel the present, past, or future physical and emotional states of people, places, things, and energy. Clairsentients feel energy and pick up on vibrations subconsciously. They receive psychic messages through sensing feelings rather than hearing voices or seeing images. They also pick up emotional sensations from any person, place, thing, or idea.

Clairsentience is often associated with intuition or the sixth sense. The abilities of clairsentients far exceed those of an empath's. They like an empath, can absorb feelings and ideas from a person, place, or thing, but they also get insight from these feelings about the person or what is happening. Clairsentients also pick up on the emotions of places, objects, or intangible energy. They will sense the emotions they experience during a meditation, a healing or during any interaction they have.

## Ways of developing Clairsentience

Focus on your breathing: it's important to meditate and focus on your breathing. Once you breathe correctly, and begin to meditate regularly and quiet your mind, you'll be able to develop your psychic senses faster.

Talk to your inner self and intuition: focus on your inner self and your intuition. Try thinking and meditating by focusing on the intuitive part of you within. Once you do this, you'll be able to regularly tap into your clairsentient abilities and there are energies that will begin to flow through and allow you to possess these capabilities automatically.

## Clairaudience

Along with the other psychic senses, such as clairvoyance and clairsentience, you also have clairaudience, which means 'clear hearing' and is the ability to hear other dimensions and frequencies of the spirit world.

Clairaudience can come through in an assortment of ways and it can be different for everyone, it may be one word, full on sentences, songs or even ringing noises. It is the capability of receiving an intuitive vocal message from the world of spirits or a higher being. Clairaudient people can extend their hearing to transcend the everyday physical world and the known level of awareness, in order to reach the world beyond. Clairaudients are highly intuitive people who are able to listen to a voice other than their own when the spirit world transmits a message to them.

It is more of a gift and something that simply comes to people. People are clairaudient by nature and begin hearing noises or voices come to them or can get symbols and messages through sounds, noises, music, ringing noises, or even messages from people they knew who have passed.

Some signs you could be a clairaudient are: ringing in your ears, giving advice to others often and knowing about their situation, and inspiration just comes naturally to you. Sometimes you are channeling or receiving information from higher beings of a different dimension.

## Ways of developing Clairaudience

Listen for new sounds: find a time in your home when there is no noise or any music or sounds and try to listen for any sounds around you. Open up your senses and try your best to listen to new noises or sounds that could be coming from all kinds of places around you.

Listen to your intuition: it's important to listen to your intuition. Find a quiet place to sit and listen to your inner self and your inner intuition. Try to even speak to your higher self by calling out to it. The more you hone in and tune into your intuition or the inner part of you that is psychic and exists within your energy body, the easier it will be to develop your psychic abilities and make them better than they currently are.

Meditate regularly: Mediation allows you to quiet your mind and focus on the sounds around you. This focused attention could help you really tap into your clairaudient abilities. Once you quiet your mind, your psychic abilities can develop a lot easier. There are many different ways to meditate such as guided meditations or sitting quietly and focusing on your breathing. It's good to find the best method that works for you.

## Clairvoyance

Clairvoyance is the psychic sense that allows you to see or perceive events or occurrences that will happen in the future. Clairvoyance is a very special gift to have and there are many people out there who do have this ability, and they utilize the best they can to help benefit their life or just for knowledge, in order to know which path to take in their life and world.

Clairvoyance is the ability to perceive information that is not known to others or that is beyond the range of ordinary perception. It is a type of extrasensory perception ESP. Fortune tellers who read people's futures practice clairvoyance.

Synonyms of clairvoyance include second sight and sixth sense. There are many people out there who possess this ability, and it is the ability to receive information that would normally be considered impossible to get through scientifically proven sensations.

## Ways of developing Clairvoyance

Focus on your inner self and intuition: It is important to focus on your inner self and intuitive abilities. This means talking to your higher self and inner self. Your higher self is the part of you that exists outside of this realm, and it exists in a higher dimension, yet you have complete access to it. Your higher self can assist you with opening up your clairvoyant abilities. Also silently talking to your intuitive self can allow you to become more psychically Intune and develop your abilities and is an ability in itself. Your higher and inner self can also give you information internally in order to be able to know things about a person's life, past, present or future.

Meditation: Meditation can help with developing any kind of psychic abilities and being able to meditate regularly will allow you to open up your chakras and your third eye chakra and further develop your psychic abilities

Visualization: Try visualizing someone's future or their life. Once you've opened up your third eye chakra and your abilities and energies have become more developed, you can easily just look at a person and look into their future and naturally be able to perceive their future and these abilities such as clairvoyance will come to you. Try visualizing someone's future, or their past and determine if you're able to psychically perceive their situation or life.

## Claircognizance

Claircognizance is the intuitive ability to understand or know something without any prior knowledge or reasoning. It's often described as a clear knowing or insight that comes to someone all of a sudden. People can receive information or answers out of the blue and know that all of these things are in fact certain. It is having a strong sense of knowing something without any real logic behind it.

## Ways of developing Claircognizance

Meditation: Meditation helps quiet the mind regularly and helps a person enhance their intuitive abilities.

Ask questions: If you ask questions to the universe and are open to receiving answers, then a lot of the time you will be given that information on its own and sometimes automatically once you begin this process.

Journaling: If you keep a journal to record your thoughts, feelings, and insights, or any intuitive feelings you experience you can easily refer back to the journal to look into these experiences and further develop them. Journaling is a key way to help understand how these concepts work and to develop any psychic abilities.

## The importance of energy and how it speaks to us.

Energy is an important part of our life and world, and we live our lives through energy and energetic interactions that occur in our everyday and momentary interactions with one another on this planet and in general through our presence and existence in the universe. It's important to learn how to use your energy and psychic gifts to shield yourself against psychic vampire and psychic attacks of any kind and to be a person who tries their hardest to eliminate and eradicate a psi vampire from your life completely.

## How to use your psychic gifts.

Your psychic gifts are your spiritual abilities and gifts that are held near and dear to you that exist somewhere within your true nature and spirit. Most or many people have some form of psychic abilities within themselves. Many people out there do not believe in the concept of psychic abilities and feel as if the concept doesn't exist, is bogus, or is some kind of mythical fairy tale, though they do exist.

## How to sense energy in others

It's not that difficult to be able to sense energy in other people. In order to be able to guard yourself against a psychic vampire, you will need to know how to read people's energies. This is something that came naturally to me once I spiritually awakened. I began to notice people's energy signatures and could notice people's energies and what kind of energies they had within them. This is something that anyone can really do. You'll have to know what energy is at first. So, what exactly is energy within a person? Energy is the life force and aura of a particular given person that has incarnated on this planet earth. Everyone has their own specific type of energy inside of their body, and their own unique aura. In order to be able to read energy in people, you'll have to have some kind of psychic gift of insight and will need to know exactly how to see and perceive this energy in others.

In order to read energy, you'll have to know how to see, perceive and sense it first. Do you know anything about your own energy? Have you ever examined your own energy and know what color it is, what type it is? You will also need to look at people's bodies and be able to read the energy associated with their body. The way to do this is by looking at people and noticing the energy associated with them and beginning to do this regularly so that it becomes something automatic. Once you do this and it's automatic, you'll learn to easily read people's energies.

You'll have to go deep within the energies in your sacral chakra and your pituitary gland to be able to do this, or just use the superficial energy that surrounds you, though it's something that you can sense or know or something that becomes automatic. Once you go deep within your chakras to be able to read energies, it activates other energies and allows you to be able to further use your spiritual and intuitive gifts more effectively.

This is also something you can do using your inner and intuitive self, your higher self and through your third eye chakra. What is the third eye chakra? It is the chakra located between your eyes set on the temple of your forehead. Once this chakra is activated, you can easily be able to see and read people's energies.

If you want to activate your third eye chakra, you'll need to just rub on it or tap it and attempt to activate it this way.

## Ways of activating the third eye chakra can include:

## Meditation

Sit in meditation and focus on visualizing a symbol, like an eye or bright light, in the center of your forehead. Regular meditation can strengthen your third eye and help you develop a stronger sense of intuition.

## Sun gazing

Gazing at the sun at dawn or dusk can activate your third eye. You can also chant "Om" while sun gazing, as the vibration of the chant matches the frequency of this chakra.

## Sound healing

Use sound healing techniques like Tibetan singing bowls or chanting. This can often open up the third eye chakra

## Creative pursuits

Journaling, creating art, or making a movie can stimulate your third eye chakra.

## Crystals

Some people believe that crystals like amethyst and lapis lazuli can help open the third eye.

## Epsom salt

Take a bath or shower with Epsom salts and rub the salt on your forehead to open your third eye.

## Grounding exercises

Sit in a chair and push your feet into the floor to release energy. Meditate while grounding yourself as well.

Once you've activated your third eye chakra, you should be able to easier sense and read people's energies. People's energies will become more apparent to you, and you will be able to know people, read deeper into them and who they are, and be able to sense the type of energy that they harbor within themselves.

## How to psychically read people's lives and aspects about them.

Reading people or doing readings on people can be simple once you learn, but initially can be a little bit challenging to have to partake in. With a little bit of practice, you'll be able to read people's energies and read them psychically using your own innate psychic abilities. Now who has psychic abilities? Most people do possess psychic abilities but haven't had the resources or knowledge to tap into them or do not have the desire to do this.

Reading a person literally comes from being able to energetically sense and know about a person using your psychic abilities. You'll have to focus on the corner of your face and temple and third eye chakra and outside of yourself to the left in order to be able to utilize the ability to read people and this is only one way or method. After activating your third eye chakra, you should be able to sense energy in some form.

## How to shield yourself from psychic vampires.

There are many different ways to shield yourself from psychic vampires. Psychic vampires are very adamant and determined creatures and they'll usually want to target a person if they have no shield. If people have a shield or a way to thwart a psi vampire, they'll be less likely to take advantage of that person. You'll want to build upon your spiritual and psychic abilities as well by learning various and even advanced techniques when it comes to how to handle or deal with an energy vampire. These techniques will allow you to be able to fight an energetic attack and even protect yourself energetically. There are other ways you can also learn to take your power back, remove the vampire from your life, and gain power and strength rather than letting this creature take your life force from you or continue to take advantage of you.

## Set firm boundaries

It's important to set boundaries with an energy vampire. You'll need to tell or show them that you're the one in charge and that they have no right or reason to be anywhere near you or to hurt or harm you in any manner. When you create a new boundary, you are communicating to others what behaviors are okay and what's *not* okay.

Without boundaries in place, energy vampires will take over and have free reign over our time and energy. They will feel as if they are free to do what they want to do with you and they enjoy the power they hold over another person or even the pain or suffering they cause another person.

## Cleanse the energy of your space

Another way you can help yourself when it comes to energy vampires and attacks is by cleansing the energy of your space. This can be done different ways through smudging an herb called sage and getting sage sticks. This protects and helps heal and cleanse your home and personal areas of any negative energies around. This also helps to remove any toxic residue leftover by an energy vampire.

## Use cord-cutting meditations

There is often a cord attached to you and others when it comes to negative interactions and it's important to find a healthy meditation that will allow you to cut the cords between you and other negative people in your life. This can help clear any issues or unresolved problems that are ongoing or happening. These meditations also clear any negative energy and help protect you in the future.

### Be love and light and true to yourself

Staying true to yourself and focusing on being greater love and light and being the good, positive person you are can assist you with dealing with negative circumstances and especially an energy vampire. The more love and goodness you put out into your world, the less negative people and vampires will want to invade it. The reason negative vampires choose empaths to target is because of the large amounts of energy they possess and the type of positive energy they have. If you continue to pursue being love, it can help with ridding yourself of an energetic parasite.

### Use the power of crystals to help and heal

Crystals are amazing conduits of energy, and they can help people from psychic attacks in various forms. There are many crystals out there that can aid and assist a person when it comes to energetic vampire attacks. Some popular ones include black tourmaline, citrine, black obsidian, red garnet, and amethyst.

### Call upon your higher self

Sometimes your higher self can actually aid and assist you in certain situations. You should call upon your higher self and God in a situation like this asking for help in a psychic vampire attack and to deal with any given situation. What is your higher self? Your higher self is the part of you that has unlimited wisdom, knowledge and knows everything about your soul and what you have ever encountered in your life. It knows how to guide you throughout your life journey and can assist and aid you in troubling times.

The higher self is the most enlightened version of you, it is free from ego and holds universal truths. It's not separate from you and operates on a higher level of consciousness. It embodies peace and wisdom and offers you unlimited wisdom and guidance.

It is a calm, loving, and spiritual guide that brings our positive characteristics to the surface and tasks us with questioning our lower nature.

Our Higher Self knows our true purpose and encompasses our potential to live a fulfilling and joyous life through personal growth and self-awareness.

## The use of essential oils

The use of essential oils can be of great benefit to those who are dealing with energy vampires. Lavendar and other oils are supportive against energy vampires. Other oils are tea tree and frankincense, the oil of truth.

You can use essential oils to apply to specific chakras, diffuse as needed, or apply to the bottoms of your feet or the insides of your wrists.

# Chapter 10

# THE EMPATH'S WAY OF LIFE

Empaths live a life of being one and in tune with others, with nature and with life and those around them. The empath lives a life of humbleness, oneness and is appreciative of those around them. Empaths enjoy being humble, kind people and love giving energy to others and healing them in different ways. The Empath is a very kind soul and lives a life of wanting to help others and heal them.

Empaths hold the key to many different things in life. An empath carries with them an inner peace and beauty that no one can imagine, and they live life carrying a torch of wanting to do good to others and help others in their own journeys in life, as well as increasing the positivity and good in their own life's journey. The empaths manner of living in a blessed one and they do what they can to live a life of fulfillment and enjoy being in the moment and enjoy life's journeys and each and every beautiful aspect of life and the given world.

An empath is caring and giving and does what it can to give of his or herself to others.

An empath holds goodness near and dear and will do anything in their power to be of helpful and good nature towards others. Empaths are natural healers and have natural abilities. Empaths live in a constant nature of being in tune with others and one with nature and the world. To be a person who is a giver is to be a special kind of person who enjoys the enjoyment of others and living in peace with others. Empaths are very sensitive people who enjoy the company of others but often prefer to be alone to recharge their energies.

The dream of the empath is to be a driven, spiritually awakened person who does good and helps and heals others and lives a life of goodness and happiness and blessing all around around him or her. They usually eat a variety of high vibrational foods, and what they eat is akin to what helps or assists them with keeping up with their high vibrations. They often do not eat junk foods, high fats, or foods that can damage or hurt their aura or energy body.

Empaths are very serious about their love of wanting to do good for the greater of humanity and work for the good of others. They are beautiful, caring, kind people and you'll find them in a variety of fields and especially in healing modalities.

They are sensitive souls who not only empathize with what others are feeling but actually feel others' emotions, energy and sometimes physical symptoms in their own bodies. They also feel their own emotions and feelings more strongly than the average person. Negativity tends to overwhelm them, as do crowds and other people in general. They can have highly addictive personalities throwing themselves into an activity or pastime to escape the energies around them. Empaths are often very good listeners and know how to treat friends and family members fairly.

The empath lives a life of being an extremely sensitive, caring intuitive person who is constantly using their intuitive and spiritual abilities to aid those around them energetically and psychically without people's knowledge. People can often become healed from an empath just from their very interaction with one and not even know it.

Empaths are extremely sensitive people who need to learn how to protect themselves and their energies. They are very high energy people who are bombarded with a host of varying universal and spiritual energies and are often lightworkers who do work on this planet to help and heal others.

# Empaths and their intuition

Empaths possess a great and grand intuition and use their intuitive abilities to aid them with spiritual processes and many other things associated with life and everyday things in their world. Empaths are naturally gifted healers and intuitives who can sense many different things and who harbor great skills.

Empaths possess a heightened intuition and use their intuition for many different purposes during their healing sessions and in many other ways as well.

Empaths hold a gift when it comes to how they use their intuitive skills. They generally are characterized by having healing abilities they use to heal other people's lives and can perform a variety of healing techniques. Empaths can be clairsentients, clairvoyants and generally have many different kind of abilities within themselves. Indigos and Crystals are special kinds of empaths

They have a keen sense of intuition and know how to use their amazing abilities on others and in this world. They connect to other beings by channeling their energies naturally and have the ability to do this on a regular and automatic basis. Empaths are incredibly special people and there are different types of them out there including the indigo and crystal people, and those who are spiritually inclined.

# Indigo empaths

Indigo empaths are very special and spiritual people. They are known as 'star humans', and belong in a group of people along with crystal and rainbow children or people. These star people possess an innate deep love for the spiritual, have natural and heightened spiritual abilities, and are on this planet for a very special reason and a purpose.

Star children are very special spiritual individuals that potentially originated from far-distant planets, solar systems, and galaxies. Many are believed to have lived many lives within other star systems far away from our own. There are several different types of Starseed children and they harness a very special purpose on this planet. They are here to bring peace, topple corrupt systems, and shift dimensional consciousness.

They have a special responsibility to assist in the rebirth of a higher-dimensional better, peaceful and greater Earth that is free of evils, corruption, and anything associated with negativity. They have a strong desire to remove these corrupt systems and change the way the world is.

The Indigo empath is one who has a high sense of morals, standards and integrity. They tend to dislike people who have egos or who are very arrogant. They are in need of stimulation and have a host of energies within them and need to partake in activities in order to handle these energies. They do things they enjoy and enjoy living life and understand the meaning and true beauty and reason for life and the blessings of being on this planet and of life.

These empaths carry a very special purpose on this planet, along with being able to illuminate the planet with their gracious and wonderful energies and carry with them a purple or indigo aura. They also need to learn how to protect themselves energetically simply because they are prone to being targeted by energy vampires regularly due to their very high energy and positive spiritual nature.

Indigo Empaths are intuitive, sensitive, and very creative people. They use their creative outlets in a host of areas such as painting, singing, writing and are gifted and have many different talents. Many want to change the system and want change to happen for the benefit of all of humanity and want to create a better world for everyone.

## Crystal empaths

Crystal empaths are very similar to indigo empaths. Crystal children are very special children and people who hold many spiritual gifts. Born after 2001, these earthy, peacemaking children are specifically here to make the world a better place and to change the world for good. These people are called crystal children and possess, and their high vibration is dominant around their crown chakra, which is like a pure white crystal chakra.

Crystal children possess special spiritual gifts and are often diagnosed with autism or on the autism spectrum. Crystal children are unique in their ability to say what's on their minds and bring light, love, and joy to others.

Crystal children deserve to be respected and understood. Their connection to the spiritual realm is something that we can't fully understand. Crystal children know who they are inside. Their confidence is a light to others.

Advocating for love and peace on Earth, Crystal children may have gifts of clairvoyance and healing. Crystal children are believed to bring up humanity and many work for a greater cause for the better benefit of the world.

You can be moved to your highest self when you see a Crystal child channel their healing energy through art, music, and the way that they love. They often want to be teachers to everyone around them and teach people about the ways of being spiritual and the gifts they behold. They have the ability to influence others to be who they truly are.

Crystal children are
In tune with their inner voice
Have no need to manipulate others
Many are autistic or in this spectrum
They are physically and mentally sensitive
They express themselves through music and singing
They are very honest and love family and friends
They have a strong physical response to negative events

# Rainbow Empaths

Rainbow children are usually born by Crystal children from the late 1980s. They have come here to help heal the earth and humanity.

They are quick to recover from negative emotions and have the same qualities and traits as crystal children. They are able to read people's feelings making them psychic. They also have a natural draw to color.

Their aura holds are few more spectrum of different ray colors. They are born with a huge heart and bring joy and love to their families and are natural gifted healers. They possess psychic abilities and can read people and their feelings. They have a unique and strong connection to color and are drawn to wearing colorful clothes. You can even experience divinity by looking into the eyes of a rainbow child. They are loving and giving, very caring people, possess bravery, and are telepathic in nature.

Empaths are highly gifted intuitive special and very spiritual people. Energy vampires are at the total opposite end of this spectrum. The empath is ages different from the energy vampire, and yet the empath often finds him or herself at the mercy of the energy vampire who will always pick or choose the empath as a victim of their energetic stealing ways. The reason the energy vampire chooses the empath is because of the empath's amazing spiritual gifts and abilities and their amazing high energy they possess because they are extremely gifted, talented individuals who are constantly channeling energies automatically due to their very natures. They usually carry with them an abundance of energy, and the energy vampire perceives them as the perfect target due to their high nature of having an abundance of readily accessible energy.

As a result, the empath finds themselves at the whim of the energy vampire, sometimes constantly depleted or having to fight and struggle to survive and rid themselves of this energy vampire or having to constantly find ways to protect themselves from these very negative and toxic people. The empath is a beautiful, special amazing spiritual creation who exists solely to help and heal others, while the energy vampire is there simply to ruin or destroy the empath because of the great qualities he or she does possess. The energy vampire also harbors a jealousy of the empath because of the great qualities and energies they have. The empath and non-empath need to find and learn ways to protect themselves from this dangerous and negative energy vampire and learn how to thwart and stop it from its evil ways towards them.

Negative vampires are often hindered by people who can fight back against them and can and will easily give up for they are generally on the attack for easy prey and an easy quick fix to their own energy issues and problems. Since most people out there are not aware of the problem of energy vampires, it's easy for one to attack most unprotected unsuspecting victims, but if there is someone out there armed with the knowledge and abilities about these predators, then they will move onto a different prey.

It's important for an empath and any person to be able to avoid and protect themselves from an energy vampire and people need to learn how to protect themselves. Hopefully you have learned the different kinds of vampires that exist out there, how they function what they do, and how to survive and deal with a vampire, and the many ways you can elevate your own abilities and use them to help protect yourself against any kind of spiritual attack or any form of psychic attack. Once you learn these effective techniques and tactics, you're well on your way to becoming a powerhouse that can easily thwart any negative vampire attacks and who can constantly protect yourself against any form of evil or negative psychic attacks towards you.

www.ingramcontent.com/pod-product-compliance
Lightning Source LLC
LaVergne TN
LVHW012053070526
838201LV00083B/4506